ENCOUNTERS
ON THE ASTRAL

ISBN 1-872189-24-5

I-H-O BOOKS

© 2000,
Essex House, Thame, England. OX9 3LS.

ENCOUNTERS ON THE ASTRAL

Dedication

To all those, seen and unseen

Who are seeking the way

CONTENTS

FOREWORD

I have known Chris since he was first commissioned to write an article about his "out of the body" experiences, for my *Encounters* magazine, and have subsequently encouraged him on more than one occasion to consider writing a book on the subject. So, I am glad to see that, in his own words, he finally got down to doing it. Although there are many books now available on the subject, some of Chris's experiences would appear to be unique to him, and are a real eye-opener to the possibilities as to what may be out there! I feel sure that this small but extremely informative account of Chris's Astral encounters will be of great interest to both, those new to this field, and those who consider themselves to be well read on the subject. I personally found the book to be fascinating from beginning to end, and look forward to any further writing that he may do on the subject.

Uri Geller
www.urigeller.com

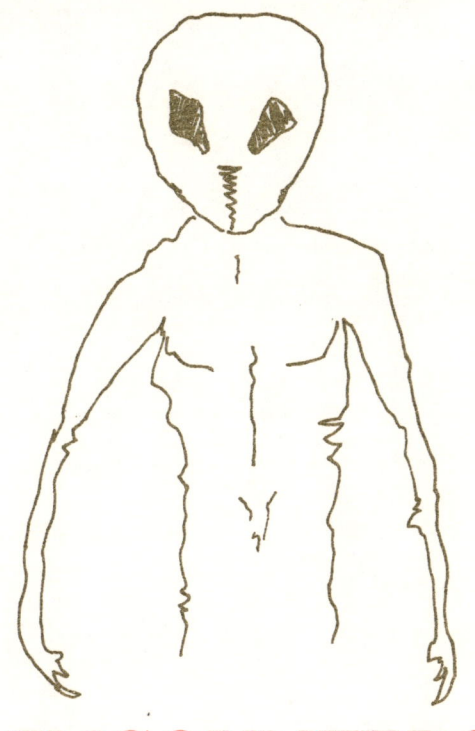

ENCOUNTERS

ON THE ASTRAL

A PERSONAL RECORD OF
OUT OF BODY EXPERIENCES

BY

CHRIS BURROWS

INTRODUCTION

It's 1.05 pm on Sunday the 16th of July 2000, and I am at long last sitting down and starting to document some of the many "out of the body experiences" that I have had over the last 47 years.

Although I have been interviewed on numerous occasions over the years by various magazines and TV programmes, it's only now, after the support from my publishers Mandrake Press, and the encouraging letters, e-mails and phone calls from folk who have read previous articles that I am finally getting on with it.

As there have been so many astral journeys made by me over the years it would be unfair of me to try to document them all in this book. Unfair for two reasons, firstly, the book would be so big and heavy that you would probably risk doing yourself an injury lugging it about, and secondly, many of the experiences, especially in the early years, were very repetitive and would only get in the way, or even, dare I say it Bore you!

I have decided that, after I have given you a brief outline of the circumstances that seemed to spark off my experiences, the best way forward is to take you through my astral projections by dividing them up into three different sections, firstly, covering those projections in which I was not fully conscious, and unable to do anything more than observe my surroundings from an almost paralyzed state. Secondly, covering some of the journeys that I made outside the body, completely separated from my physical other half and fully conscious. Then, thirdly, I will introduce you, as it were, to some of the beings that I have encountered whilst travelling on the astral plane. Although these beings which I have moved among bear a strong resemblance to the so-called aliens from space that other people claim to have encountered, it is not my theory that they are from any far off galaxy, but in fact reside far closer to home! My conclusions are of course mine and I take full responsibility for them, but I do encourage you to think for yourself, and by all means draw your own.

I should point out that the three areas of experience which I am writing about did not happen in sequence. For instance, I still to this day find myself trapped half out of my physical self and unable to move, and I first encountered other beings on the astral plane in the 70s. So, although my very early projections were more or less in a semi-conscious state, the intensity of my travels since those early days has varied considerably.

One thing I have not done is include any "how to" type instructions, the reason being that all my projection experiences came about naturally, without me having to refer to any manual of technique. I have to say though, that my many years of training in meditation practices certainly enabled me to take more control of my astral double, and if any reader is interested in trying astral travel for themselves, I heartily recommend that they start by getting some solid training in a reputable school of meditation as a basis for such esoteric work!

My experiences of astral projection started when I was a lad of five, continued through my life as a touring jazz/rock drummer and on into my life as a Buddhist monk. Some of my journeys have been frightening, some amazing, but they have all added to my insights into the human condition. To get the most out of this book I suggest you approach it with a sense of openness and adventure combined with the willingness to leave behind opinions!

From now on, to keep things simple, I will refer to my "out of the body experiences" as simply OBEs (not to be confused with medals handed out by the Queen). So sit back, read on, and as they say, let me beam you up Scotty!

HOW IT ALL STARTED

I am five years old, and my brother Michael and I are being walked home from school in St Albans, England, by my mother, it's the 16th of February 1954, it's cold and although its only around 3.30 in the afternoon it is winter and it is already getting dark.

Apparently, according to my mother who was always able to remember this incident with far more clarity than me, I had always been, up till now that was, a very quiet and well-behaved child. But, for no reason that she could figure out, when we were about half way home I started to cry and scream, and eventually sat on the ground and refused point blank to go any further. My mother was so embarrassed by this out of character outburst that she offered to make a short detour to visit my grandmother who lived only a short distance from where we were, but only if I stopped my dreadful behaviour!

The thought of visiting my grandmother's instead of going home had the effect of subduing me instantly and we trotted off in the direction of her house. I didn't really understand my fear of returning to my own home, but as you will see from the events that followed, it was based on a premonition that was to save my life! Grandmas being what they are the world over, it was insisted upon that we all stay to tea, and it was eventually 7 p.m. before we set off to continue our journey home, me having completely forgotten my earlier panic attack.

I was only five years old and 7 o'clock was my bedtime, so, by rights I should have been tucked up in bed by now!

Just as we left my grandmother's house there was a loud crash of what sounded like thunder, plus an accompanying downpour of hailstones. Fearing a storm, my mother hurried us along towards home. Very soon a fire engine zoomed past with it's bell ringing, and my brother and I shouted with joy at the sight of it, only to arrive home and discover that it was our house that was in flames!

After all the commotion died down my mother was informed by the fire-officer that the house had not been hit by lightening but by the remains of a meteorite, or what some folk called a thunderbolt. The meteorite had gone through not only the roof of our house but also right through my bed! The same bed, that had it not been for my out of character fit, I would have actually been in at the time of impact! Obviously, the thunderous sound that we heard and assumed was an impending storm was the meteorite entering the earth's atmosphere.

We went to live with my grandmother for a short time while the local council, who owned our fire damaged property, had it repaired and redecorated. Then, after a while, we moved back in, and I started sleeping in my brand new bed, although I have to say I never really did feel quite right in my newly acquired piece of furniture. One aspect that I found a little unnerving was the fact that even though the council had re-wallpapered my bedroom, there was still a dark line on the wall that came down from the ceiling and ended by the side of my bed, a line that I assumed had been caused by the meteorites burning entry. I was also somehow aware, as I lay in bed on those first few evenings, that my premonition sparked bout of bad behaviour was in some way linked with the meteorite, and by rights I probably shouldn't be alive!

SEMI CONSCIOUS PROJECTIONS

I think I have probably written enough by way of an introduction to my experiences, and you are more than likely starting to think "yes, come on, get on with it", so without further ado I will now take you through a few of my earlier OBEs. Purely on the basis of simplicity I will just list them in numerical order, starting with, as far as I am aware, my first projection.

PROJECTION 1

It must have been a couple of nights after we moved back into our house that I was to have this first experience, although I didn't know at the time that it was an OBE, and it wasn't until I read a book on the subject some years later that all of this made sense to me.

I had gone to bed as normal and had dropped of to sleep fairly quickly as I always did, and still do. I have no idea how long I had been asleep or indeed any idea what time it would have been, but I suddenly found myself awake, but in a way that I had not experienced before, and in fact I still remember feeling a little scared. I was lying on my back, in a state that I thought was fully conscious, but I could not see, even though I was under the impression that my eyes were open. It was very dark and uncomfortably still, and I lay there for a short time before I started to try to move. Panic really set in when I found that I was paralyzed and couldn't move any part of my body, firstly trying to move my arms, then trying to sit up, then trying to move my eyes from side to side in order to take in some familiar aspect of my bedroom, but no matter how hard I tried I couldn't move a single muscle of my physical body.

What contributed to this being so scary was the fact that I knew that I was not dreaming, that I was somehow in a semi-conscious state but unable to physically function. How long I lay there trying to move I have no idea, but after a time the panic became more intense and I found myself thinking about my mother and trying to shout out her name. I soon found out, of course, that trying to shout out loud was just as difficult as trying to move my limbs, but I persevered for what seemed like a very long time until eventually, I thought that I could hear my own voice calling out. Suddenly I awoke with a jolt and sat up sharply in the bed. I sat there for a while feeling a little disorientated, and noticed that I had sweat pouring down my face. Then my mother burst through the door with a look of concern on her face, and a voice to match. She had heard my shouting out for her as she sat downstairs with my father, and explained that my voice seemed to get louder and louder and ended with a final very loud outburst of the word "mummy" which must have been the one final shout that also brought me back from my semi-projected state. My mother comforted me for a while, trying to reassure me with the explanation that it had just been a bad dream, then left me to go back to sleep.

I lay there for some time before I eventually dropped off again, a little worried that there would be some sort of recurrence of my experience. The next morning I gave very little thought to my seeming nightmare, and as it was not mentioned by my mother, I assumed that it was a one off. How wrong I was! This OBE was, as I would soon discover, only the beginning of many more to come, the next being only a few days later.

Reflecting for a moment on my mother's comments that my experience had been a bad dream, it's funny, but even to this day, after nearly fifty years of having OBEs, some people still say to me "it must just be a bad dream". Why is it I wonder that so many people are afraid of anything remotely esoteric? If they want to know what a bad dream is, all they have to do is take a look at the human condition!

Projection 2

As mentioned, I did indeed have another very similar OBE to my first one just a few days later, plus a few more of the same intensity over a period of a couple of months. But then after a while, just as I was getting used to them, as it were, things started to hot up a bit. This second projection that I am going to take you through is a sort of next stage in my level of awareness.

I was laying on my back, fast asleep as usual and obviously totally oblivious to what time it was, when, as had by now happened quite a few times, I found myself becoming conscious of my surroundings but still, or so it seemed, in a state of sleep.

What was to make this a little different to my previous OBEs was that I was suddenly aware that I had vision, that I could actually make out various aspects of my bedroom. I tried to move my head to look around but it was just an impossible task, so I just scanned as wide as I could by moving my eyes from side to side and up and down. If I had in any way considered my previous experiences to be just dreams, this new heightened awareness of my surroundings confirmed that what I was experiencing was no dream, I was awake, all be it unable to move any of my limbs, but very aware of being on my bed and in my own familiar room. The next thing that started to dawn on me as I lay there was that there was no colour, everything was in a sort of black and white, or to be more exact a kind of sepia, a bit like those old photographs that you see in your grandmother's photo album or in the museum.

It seemed like I lay there for quite a long time just indulging in my newly acquired visual skill, all the while feeling both elated and scared. Although I was now far more conscious of my surroundings than on any previous OBE, I could hear no sounds, and was somehow aware, for some reason, that I was sweating a lot. But after some time I just drifted back into my normal sleep mode and woke the next morning with a very clear and lucid memory of the evenings events. Again, as with my earlier experiences, this new level of visually aided projection was to recur many times over the next year or so, in fact it became so common place that, I hate to say it, I became almost blasé about it all.

I think I was about seven years old when things started to intensify again, and if I had been at all blasé on previous occasions I certainly would never be blasé again. Read on and all will be revealed!

Projection 3

I had not been having any OBEs for some months, or certainly none that I was in anyway conscious of, when one evening I found myself in one of my usual astraly awake states, unable to move but with that sepia toned vision that came with my more recent experiences. But, after lying still for a short time, I became aware of what I can only call a presence, I felt sure that someone was in the room with me, and that they were very close. My brother shared my bedroom and would have been asleep in the bed on the other side of the room, but I knew it was not him, it was something else. I had felt a little scared in the past during my projections, but what I felt now was more like fear! I felt panic setting in, and was aware that once again I was sweating profusely. I moved my eyes around the room desperately trying to see who was there, I was also trying with all my might to move physically, when suddenly, completely unexpectedly I sat up in bed, my astral body from the waist up was actually sitting up in bed. After just sitting still for a while trying to take in what had happened I started to look around, I looked down and could see my blanket covered legs directly in front of me, I could move around from my waist up in just the same way that I would do if it were my physical body. I then remembered my feeling of fear brought about by the awareness of someone else in the room and started to scan the room for any sign of some sort of ghostly being, but to no avail, there was no one there, and the feeling of any presence had also gone.

I then started to feel very tired, and felt myself slowly falling backwards into my physical body, which I found very relaxing, until, what must have been the moment that my astral body fully aligned with its physical counterpart when I felt a terrible shock that woke me instantly from my sleep and left me lying on the bed totally exhausted. I lay there for some time trying to come to terms with what I had just experienced until I finally fell asleep. When I woke up the next morning I was still feeling exhausted, I was totally shattered and when I went downstairs for breakfast I found that I just could not eat. My mother asked me what was wrong, but I just didn't want to talk, and I never told her about the previous nights encounter. For many years I kept all my OBE experiences to myself and only talked to my mother about them in later years, only to find, surprisingly, that she believed every word I told her, and was in fact quite fascinated by the subject!

I think the three variations of what I term my "semi-conscious projections" that I have just gone through are enough to paint a clear picture of what was happening, and from the age of five years to the age of eleven years old I had many mixed versions of them all.

Things started to change again though when I was eleven years old, and just a month after we had moved into a new house. There was nothing wrong with the old one, but my father was doing well in business and although we were all happy in our old house, he was convinced that we would be even happier if we moved up market and into our own privately owned home. Some people never learn! Anyway, for better or for worse, the move turned out to be a step up the astral social ladder for me as the move seemed to trigger off a new phase in experiences.

FULLY CONSCIOUS PROJECTIONS

What I mean by fully conscious projections is when my astral double actually breaks away completely from my physical body rather than just observing my surroundings from an almost paralysed state, or, at the most, just being able to sit up in bed, as it were, with my astral upper half. In these full projections I was able to move around at will, and travel anywhere that I wished in a fully conscious and fully focused state of mind. The best way to give you an idea of what these journeys were like is probably to take you through a few of them, so here is, as far as I can remember, my first astral walkabout.

JOURNEY 1

The first month in our new home was very much a settling in period, and the fact that it was a brand new house meant that no one else had been there before us. This of course allowed us the privilege of being able to create our own personal safe haven, and I feel sure that it was this feeling of having a place that was in a way sacred to us that my projections started again with a whole new intensity. So, one evening, approximately four weeks after our move, sometime after falling asleep I found myself in the, by now, not unfamiliar situation of being awake in my astral body, and just lying there taking in the feel of the room. But it soon started to dawn on me that something was different, even allowing for the fact that this was the first OBE that I had consciously experienced in this house. I then realised that the ceiling was closer to me, as if it had dropped a few feet and was just above my face. But then as I started to glance around me I felt a sudden shock go right through me when I realised that it was not the ceiling that was closer to me, but me that had risen up off the bed and was hovering in mid air. As I looked down it seemed to trigger off a new kind of movement and I found myself floating down towards the floor, feet first, until I came to rest standing next to my brother's bed. I could see him curled up and fast asleep, and I stood there for a while just looking at him until I felt the desire come over me to turn round and look at my own bed. I am not sure what I was expecting to see but I could almost feel my astral jaw drop as I saw myself still lying there, flat on my back and seemingly fast asleep. After a few moments I decided to walk over and take a close look at my body, and this I did with amazing ease, although I was going through the motion of walking, I seemed to glide effortlessly across the room until I was stood looking at my own body on the bed. As I stood there, I also started to look around the room, until my eyes fell on the window just a few feet along from my bed, and as they did I started to turn and move in that direction. I never got to the window though, just as I was about to draw level with it I felt a sensation of falling come over me combined with a sort of drowsiness, and as this feeling became more intense I felt one of those dreadful shudders that I was to experience many more times in the future, and I woke from my sleep with a shout (I can't remember what I shouted) and just lay there exhausted and saturated with sweat. I can remember this first full OBE very clearly, yes, apart from the shout, almost as if it had only happened yesterday! Maybe I should point out at this stage that when I was moving around my bedroom the light was just as before, a sort of sepia tone, not colour and not black and white, and that's what it always has been up to this day, whether I am travelling around inside a building or outside in the open, or indeed whether it is night time or day time! I mention this because later on I was to have OBEs during my periods of meditation that I was undertaking during the day.

Although this full OBE that I have just taken you through was my first, I have had many, many more just like it over the years, projecting no further than a few feet from my physical body. OBEs are totally unpredictable, and although you can develop a certain amount of skill with regard to controlling them, you just never know when they are going to happen. Anyway, let's now take a look at another OBE that was very different.

JOURNEY 2

I have discovered over the years, that although there are many conditions that can contribute to having an OBE, tiredness is definitely one of the main culprits.

And it was this condition that brought about the experience that I am now going to take you through. Jumping forward a bit in time, it's the 70s and I am on tour in my role as drummer with "Arthur Browns Kingdom Come" who were a well known rock band of the time, and before you start jumping to the conclusions of, oh yes, rock bands, drugs! booze! that's what caused his OBEs, I never was interested in drugs, and by this time in my life I was well into Buddhist practice and was not drinking any alcohol! What I think contributed to my exhaustion at this time was the fact that the tour we were on was fairly gruelling, and I just had not been eating enough of the right foodstuffs to cater for the lifestyle. So it was that one evening during a tour of France the band decided, just as we were arriving in Paris, to stop and get a meal. But as I was feeling very tired I suggested that they go and eat without me, and I would curl up on the back seat of the band bus and get some sleep. When they had all disembarked, I found a seat and lay down on my right side, and as far as I can remember, fell asleep almost immediately. I can't have been asleep very long when I suddenly woke up with a start, but was instantly aware that it was my astral double that was awake and not my physical self! As I lay there on my right side just staring straight ahead, my astral double started to roll off the seat that I was lying on, and I fell downward and right through the floor of the van and onto the Paris road directly under the bus. I just lay there on the road in a state of utter confusion, I had never left my body in this way before, I had always floated upward from my body, this method of departure was just all new to me! Although I knew that this was one of my fully conscious projections and that I could, if I wished, start to move about and investigate the area I decided not to. I was unsure of myself and a little afraid that if I wondered off, I may not be able to get back to my body. I lay there on the road like some sort of astral drunk, just taking in the sounds. I could hear lots of traffic of course, and the voices of people talking in French (obviously) as they passed up and down the pathway next to the bus, then after a while I heard the familiar sound of English voices that seemed to be getting closer and closer.

This was of course the rest of the band and our two personal roadies returning from their European nosh up. The familiar sound of their voices was a trigger that sent my astral body straight back with great force into my physical, a force that was much greater than I had ever experienced on previous re-alignments. I was utterly exhausted, much more so than I had ever been before, and, although other members of the band made a few comments about the food, etc., I didn't utter a single word in reply. The feeling of being totally drained of energy lasted for nearly a week, and all of that time I don't remember carrying on a conversation about anything with anyone! Under normal conditions this lack of communication would seem like odd behaviour, but you have to remember that I was touring with a rock band with all the moods and egos, etc., that go with the job, so nobody took a blind bit of notice of my withdrawn manner. You may recollect that there was a film called *Rebel Without a Cause* well I was playing in a band without a cause! Five rebellious hippies against the world! All a bit sad when I reflect back!

If you are now ready for an OBE that was a bit more adventurous, then let me guide you through a real astral walkabout, or maybe I should say flyabout, bonanza with a third account.

Journey 3

As I said at the beginning of the book, the OBEs that I am going through with you were not necessarily experienced in the order that I am recounting them, and this next and final one under the title of "fully conscious projections" happened in the mid 60s, and is, again, only one of many of a similar intensity. At this time in my life I was living in a flat in London, but on the occasion of this particular weekend, I was visiting my parents in St Albans. It was sometime early on the Sunday morning, possibly between 1 a.m. and 3 a.m. that I found myself astraly awake and rising up from my sleeping body, just hovering for a while before slowly coming to rest standing next to my bed. By this time in the mid 60s I had been on many astral journeys, and felt no fear or apprehension about my astral detachment, plus for whatever reason, I was on this occasion feeling a little adventurous! I walked towards my bedroom door and passed straight through, which felt a bit like pushing through soft uncooked pastry. If your wondering, why uncooked pastry? well, it's because I have often been asked what it felt like passing through solid objects, and this is the closest analogy that I could come up with. Most people seem to be able to imagine in some way what I mean, although I was once asked by some smart alec of a television interviewer whether it was white or wholemeal pastry! After leaving the confines of my room I walked towards the landing window, again, passed straight through and floated gently down until coming to rest on the pathway at the side of the house. I walked towards the front garden of the house , and out into the road where I stood for a while whilst trying to decide what to do next. Due I think to my adventurous spirit at the time, I decided to try to move up into the air, up till now, although I had often left a building on the first floor, and then drifted down to ground level, I had always wondered about on the old terra firma. As corny as it may sound, the image that came to mind was that of the TV children's hero superman, who I had often watched on the goggle box as a child. So I outstretched by arms above my head in true superman fashion and willed myself up into the air, not really actually expecting anything to happen! But fly I did, and I soon found that I could control my flight with just my mind, and the superman pose, good fun as it was, was not really necessary.

I travelled upwards until I was hovering a few yards above the roof of my parents house, then after looking around a bit at the surrounding area, I literally flew around over the neighbours' roof tops before heading off towards a small clump of trees next to the main road close to the small estate that my parents' house was part of. Whilst looking down at the road, I noticed a car travelling along it, but to my surprise found that I couldn't hear its engine! I wasn't sure if this was because of my height, so I lowered myself, purely with the aid of my will to ground level, by which time the car had unfortunately disappeared out of view. But as I stood there I became very aware of not just the stillness but also of the silence. I had been out on journeys before and always heard any sounds that were in what would be normal audible distance, as in the journey I previously told you about which happened later on in the 70s in Paris, I could hear both the vehicles and the voices of people in the vicinity. But even today the same thing can happen, for some reason, I know not what, you suddenly find that you can't hear a thing, your sense of hearing just is not present during your OBE. I didn't waste too much time pondering over the absence of sound, this was my first flying experience and I was eager for more, so I willed myself into the air again, and spent what seemed like an hour or so just swooping over the rooftops of all the surrounding houses before drifting back towards my parents' house. I just pushed through the wall, as it was not really necessary to go through a window or door, I mean, who's going to tell you off for not using the front door, or not wiping your astral feet! I moved towards my own room, then as I got close to my physical body on the bed I felt the, by now, familiar sensation of going into unconsciousness as I was finally pulled back into my body in a sort of astral docking! The next morning I could recall the whole flying event with precise detail, but as with all my previous OBEs, for fear of being considered a complete nutter by my parents I kept the entire experience to myself. I did of course go on to have many more astral flyabouts, the most recent being only about a month before I sat down to write this book! The temptation being that I am living at the moment only ten minutes walk from coastal cliffs and the sea, and I find it a most invigorating area for outdoor OBEs.

I really think that the three semi projections and the three full projections that I have just guided you through are enough to give you a very good idea of what my general OBEs were like, and as I am very keen to move on to the next chapter which will describe some of the other beings that I have occasionally encountered on my journeys then I think I will do just that.

Please bear in mind what I said in the introduction! If I were to write down all my experiences, which by now are several hundred, the book would be too heavy to lug about, and could probably sink the "Titanic" (if it hadn't already been sunk that is) plus most of them were only variations of the above! So, close encounters here we come.

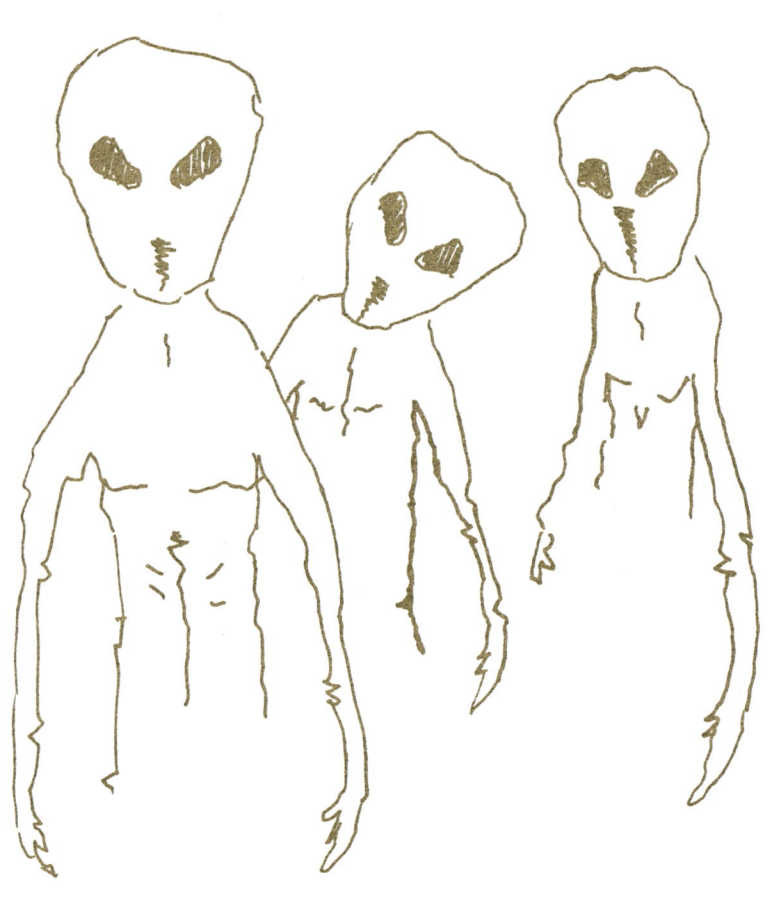

ENCOUNTERS WITH OTHER BEINGS

I f ever I am interviewed or give talks about my OBE experiences, it's this aspect that people are usually more interested in, this aspect being the other folk that I have come across on the astral plane. Apart from on one occasion, which I will tell you about first, all the beings that I encountered were of the same type as those that I have illustrated for you at the beginning of this chapter. Who or what I think they are will be covered by me in the Conclusions at the end of the book. Actually, when I say all but one, that's not entirely true!

During one OBE in the late 60s, I was standing, or should I say my astral double was standing, next to the window of my flat in London, when I became aware of a sort of energy to the left of me, I turned my head and to my utter surprise saw a dog standing next to me! This sort of astral animal was just standing there, looking in the same direction as me, just like you sometimes see dogs standing next to their owners. I turned to look around the room to see if there was anything else present, which there didn't seem to be, and when I turned to glance once more at the dog, he had disappeared. The dog was obviously on the same astral plane as me, but how or why he turned up standing next to me I just have no idea, and, up to now, it has never happen again, I have not seen another single animal during any of my OBEs.

So, leaving behind this single canine encounter, let me move on to my first encounter with, what I can only call, something!

As I said earlier, all but one of my encounters were with beings of the same type. But this one off encounter was for me a warning that I should not misuse my astral skills. It was in the mid 70s, and came about because I happened to fancy a girl who lived in the house opposite me, (sex rearing its ugly head, as my mother used to say). As on many previous occasions, I was fully projected and standing in my bedroom wondering what to do with my astral self. I made my way across to the window and glanced over to the house on the other side of the road, and then immediately thought about the girl that lived there. I had always fancied her but had never actually spoken to her, and it suddenly dawned on me that all I had to do was project myself over to her house and I could just pop into her bedroom and see her! More than once I had seen her looking out of the front bedroom window, so I knew that this was the room in the house where I would find her. I projected out of my own window and floated down to street level, then walked across to her house and, for some reason, rather than just floating upwards and through her window or wall, went through the front door. I moved up the stairs and then glanced around while I worked out which door would be hers, then I entered and walked over to the window and stared across at my own house on the opposite side of the street.

As I stood there I was very aware that the young lady of my desires was laying in the bed to my left, but for some reason I felt that I shouldn't look, for some reason it suddenly felt wrong to be there. It may have been that she was laying naked and asleep on top of the bed, I don't know, but I just felt very uncomfortable about the situation. Just as I was thinking about leaving the room I happened to glance across again to my own bedroom window opposite, and what I saw sent a cold shudder right through me!

There was something in my room, staring back at me, and although I can still to this day picture it clearly in my mind, I have not been able to illustrate it on paper, as many times as I have tried! It seemed to represent everything negative about life, everything that is evil, (for want of a better word). I stood for a while like I was frozen to the spot, just staring across at this awful entity, which just stared back in a way that made me feel like it was staring into my very being. After what seemed like a lifetime, suddenly, almost like someone had snapped their fingers, the feeling that I should return to my own physical body immediately welled up inside me with an almost terrifying urgency. As afraid as I was of coming face to face with whatever it was in my room, I shot through the young lady's wall, and without bothering with floating to ground level outside, just projected straight across to my own window, which I also moved through as if my life depended on it. You may recall how on many occasions I awoke from my OBE to find my physical body covered in sweat, well as I stood in my room it felt, for the first time, like my astral body was sweating! I could also feel my astral double almost trembling as I visually searched the room for any sign of the entity, but it had gone, and cross fingers, has not to this day returned. I have reflected back many, many times on this encounter, and am convinced that whatever it was, was drawn to me by my actions, actions that were based on selfish desires! I very much hope that the recounting of this experience will serve as a warning to any future astral travellers! Always use any skills that you may develop for good. Take it from me, the moment you start thinking about the advantages that astral travel could give you over others, you are in big trouble!

Encounter 2

Well, I guess that after the gloom and doom of the previous encounter, it would be nice for me to tell you about a couple of more positive experiences that involved meetings with the little chaps, or chapesses, (your guess is as good as mine), that you can see in my illustration. I have gone through various encounters with these beings before in previous interviews, and judging by the mail that I get, many of you out there have read about these previous encounters already. So, for all you avid readers of my experiences, here are a couple of my encounters that have never been written about before!

This particular OBE (encounter 2) took place in June 1979 in a small village in India called Savatthi. I had gone to India to visit the various locations that were associated with the Buddha, such as his birth place, the place of his enlightenment, etc., which is how I found myself in Savatthi, a small village where the Buddha and his entourage used to spend the rain seasons (monsoons). The area that the Buddha spent his time was a delightful area surrounded by trees that is just outside the village. When I arrived in 1979 there was a small Buddhist temple next to the gardens, and it's here that I was to stay for just over a week. In the centre of the original garden are the excavated remains of the buildings that the Buddha and his monks stayed in 2500 years ago. And it was here in what was, according to Ven Sangharatana the resident monk, the actual remains of the Buddha's very own quarters (actually, just a simple hut) that I used to sit morning and evening and do my meditation practice. It was on the second evening, at about 9 p.m., whilst I was sat in the gardens doing my meditation, that I found my astral double floating up from my physical body, which was sat in a contemplative cross-legged posture.

Up to this point in time, every OBE that I had experienced had been while my physical body was asleep. In case your wondering, maybe I should point out that the astral separation had nothing to do with the meditation technique that I was doing at the time, which was a practice from the Zen tradition called "Shikantaza". In fact this particular meditation is so down to earth that I find it very difficult to pass on to students, due to the fact that many find it too boring! It is of course an excellent technique, but sadly, many folk, even those looking for enlightenment, just want instant coffee, they just can't wait!

Anyway, leaving aside the actual meditation, here I was coming to rest, standing next to my cross-legged physical other half. The first thing that dawned on me was how serious and stern I looked when doing my meditation. But, after looking at myself for a short time, I suddenly had that same feeling coming over me that I had experienced on the occasion when I found a dog standing next to me in my flat in London! Then as I glanced to my right, I nearly jumped out of my astral skin when I spotted some sort of being, standing no more than two feet away, just looking at me. He had a real look of sadness about him, and unlike the previous unpleasant encounter that I told you about, I felt no fear whatsoever! Due partly to the fact that the OBE that I was experiencing had come about in a totally new way, and not while I was sleeping, I really wasn't sure what to do next. I stood for a while just staring at my visitor, who just stared back at me with his very sad eyes.

I took one more look at my own meditating body, then turned and started to walk across the gardens towards a massive Boddhi tree that stood in the centre of the grounds. All the way across I was very aware of the fact that my companion was walking with me, keeping the same distance of about two feet. He was a bit shorter than me, I am about 6 feet tall, and he came up to around my shoulders. I then spotted some more movement out of the corner of my astral eye, but when I turned to look, it was just the resident monk, Sangharatana, coming out of the temple door and going off towards one of the out buildings. He appeared to look straight at me at one point, but showed no signs of actually seeing me or my friend. I then turned and faced the visitor and tried to mouth words, but of course, nothing came out! I started to walk back over towards my physical body, and as I did I felt a pull that was a bit like when you hold a magnet near something metal. The pull became more powerful the closer I got, until, as I got within about three feet of my body, my astral double was just pulled back in, not with any kind of sudden jolt as had happened many times before, but with a refreshing gentleness. I was now back in my meditation, but fully aware of the preceding events. I sat for a while, just thinking about the being that I had encountered, wondering what or who he could have been. After about another ten minutes I decided to finish my meditation and fully opened my eyes in preparation to stand up, but that was as far as I got, for there right in front of me was not only my original visitor, but three others also!

It dawned on me immediately that I was looking at them from my physical eyes, and not from any projected astral double! I was fully awake and in the real world, yet I could see these four little fellows right in front of me. They all had the same sad look about them, almost like they had been lost for a very long time. Just as I was thinking about standing up, they all turned and walked away, and as they did, they faded, almost like they had walked into fog, and disappeared.

I had been keeping a diary of my trip to India, and that evening I recorded all the events of my encounter so that I may reflect on them later. I had no further sightings of the beings whilst I was at Savatthi, but did experience a very similar scenario later on in my trip whilst meditating in a cave just outside Pokhara, which is a small village in the Himalayan foothills. I have come into contact with, what I have come to know as my friends many times since this first encounter in India, but before I give a full account of my theories as to who they are, let me guide you through one more quite spectacular meeting with them that happened not too long ago, and only about one mile from where I am living at present.

ENCOUNTER 3

The circumstances around this particular OBE were again a little different, in that, by the time I became fully conscious in the astral and was fully aware of my surroundings, I was actually about a mile away from my sleeping body! I had gone off to bed as normal, and had no intentions of attempting to project my astral double. In fact over the last couple of years or so I have been focusing on other aspects of esoteric/occult studies and have more or less given OBEs a bit of a rest.

Be that as it may, I did project on this particular evening, and the first I knew of it was when I became fully conscious of not just the fact that I was in my astral body, but also the fact that I was standing in water, sea water to be more precise, in an area that I recognised instantly, as I had visited there with my wife and daughter on many a fossil hunting occasion. By now, after many years of OBEs, I have become quite good at judging the time of day or night that my projection was taking place, and I figured this out to be around 3 a.m. I was stood facing the cliffs, only a few yards from the shore, in water that was about 4 inches deep, the tide obviously being more or less out. Although I was familiar with the area and in no way felt threatened, I was just not feeling in anyway adventurous, and was about to do one of my superman type flights back to my house, when, seemingly out of nowhere, one of my sad looking friends suddenly appeared, standing about ten feet in front of me. Then as I glanced around me I noticed that there were more of them, about a dozen I would think, and they were circling me in a way that conjured up for me the image of a circle of standing stones! By now I had encountered these beings many times, and in no way felt any threat from their presence, in fact I always felt very privileged to be in their company. After what can only have been a few moments, a couple of them moved very cagily a little closer to me, then paused for a while before one of them moved right up to me, and stood directly in front of me for a short time, then, lifting his right arm, prodded me in the tummy area with one of his fingers. The moment his outstretched finger touched my astral body, I woke instantly, and was back in my physical body in my bed. Feeling that this encounter must have had some sort of meaning, although I knew not what, the next morning I asked my wife to drive me (I don't drive) out to the area so that I could have a walk about and try to get some sort of insight to any possible meaning. I walked across a few of the rock pools and stopped in roughly the same area that I remembered my astral double standing the night before. I glanced around, hoping I think, that I would be able to see some sign that the beings had been there, but the area was just very still, even the sea was quiet, almost like a lake. Then, just as I was about to walk back over to where my wife was patiently waiting, I happened to glance down into one of the rock pools in front of me.

There, staring up at me from the pool was a little face, a face of one of the beings! I bent down to look closer and could see that it was a rock under the water. I put my hand into the pool and lifted out the rock which was only about 2 inches across, but bare a replica of a face of one of the beings that I have been having my meetings with. It had two naturally formed indentations for the eyes, plus the raised sort of line that I always thought of as a nose, in fact, if you hold the stone up against one of the illustrations that I have made of my little friends, you would think that the stone had been deliberately modelled on them! With great enthusiasm I showed the article to my wife, and then we drove off home. I am sure that this particular meeting, combined with me finding the artefact have some meaning that I am still missing, and I often pick up the stone and carry it around with me in the hope that some insight will arise, in fact I have placed it on the computer in front of me as I type up this account of the events. This encounter happened only a couple of months ago, and I have not had any further encounters or OBEs since, so remain very open to what may be next! If anything major or earth shattering should happen in the future then I will of course offer extra material on the matter to Mandrake press, so, watch this space!

The nine varying versions of my OBEs that I have just gone through should give a very good idea of what I personally have been experiencing from the age of 5 to the ripe old age of 52. But before I finish, I would like to fill you in a little with the conclusions that I have so far drawn from it all. Then by all means draw your own!

CONCLUSIONS

As far as Astral projection itself is concerned, I have read many books by other authors on the subject, and although they are often published under the same heading of "astral projection" I think that there are probably a few variations of what people have actually been experiencing! In some cases what has been going on for folk is a form of mind projection, which is a different thing altogether, and not connected with the projection of an etheric double! But, as this book has been about the etheric form of OBEs then I am not going to go into the mind projection aspect on this occasion. Sticking then to the books about the etheric school, as it were, and based on my personal experiences over the years, I would say that where the large majority of books are genuine, I feel that some are not, and have been produced purely on the basis of making money! One American author for instance writes so enthusiastic about the power and money that you can obtain from developing the ability to astraly project, that not only do I feel that he is faking it, but I also find the approach extremely offensive!

You may of course, after reading my account of events, be coming to your own conclusions about my genuineness! Quite right! Don't just believe something because you read it in a book. One thing that I do not mention that is often talked about in other books on the subject is the silver coloured cord that is said to connect the physical body with the astral double. I am afraid that I have never seen one, sorry!

It is said that if this cord is broken while your astral double is separated from your physical then you die!

Well, the only people that would know that would be the ones that died, and they wouldn't be writing books about it would they!

Based on both my findings and those of the other trustworthy writers on the subject, I'm happy to conclude that we as humans do have an astral other half, and with practice we can develop the ability to consciously move around and investigate aspects of our life that under normal conditions remain hidden. Whether the astral double lives on after our physical body dies I do not know, but I do know that I have never seen another human being on the astral plane! You do of course see those who are still living. If I were to project my astral body into a room where there were four people, then I would see them, simple as that, but I am sorry to report that as of yet, as far as the astral plane is concerned, I have not come across a single human, dead or alive! Which brings me to the strange beings that I have encountered, and that I have become fairly familiar with. Who or what I hear you ask do I think they are? Firstly, let me dismiss any notions that they are aliens from another galaxy, as similar as they do look to those that other people say they have seen getting out of space craft. In fact, about a year ago, one of those parasitic type freelance journalists tried to talk me into saying that I had seen some of these beings coming down from an object in the sky, because we could both make some good money by selling the story to a national newspaper. I will not write down what I told him to do with his idea, as Mandrake press would probably, in the name of decency, have to edit it out!

Anyone familiar with Buddhist cosmology may come to the conclusion that they are the earthbound spirits sometimes called "Hungry ghosts" that wonder about on a different plane of existence while they wait for the negative Karma that put them there to burn out. This may be the case, and it certainly makes a lot of sense. But I have a theory that they live on that plane as its natural inhabitants, just as we are the natural inhabitants of earth's physical plane. They live alongside of us as co-habitants of this world and are probably just as confused about the meaning of life as the rest of us! One thing that worries me though, if they can see us, do they watch us when we go to the toilet? I bet that's got you worried!

I asked a friend to read through the manuscript of this book before I sent it to the publishers, just to get some sort of feedback, and his comments were that "Reading it made him feel adventurous." Well, that's good enough for me!

May all beings be free from suffering

Chris Burrows

ABOUT THE AUTHOR

WAVES
A Meditation in Sound
CB20, £11.75 CD

Using a combination of many different gongs, bells and sounds, including seven Tibetan singing bowls, Tibetan rincha and drilbu bells, Japanese bowl gongs, Chinese wind gongs and chimes plus contemporary gongs from Europe. For this recording Chris worked to the classical Indian music tradition of performing each of the four pieces at the time of day that they are intended to be listened to.

ZEN BUDDHIST CHANTING
CB22, £11.75 CD

Combining the sound of chanting with the energy of the temple drum, Chris has multi-layered his own Buddhist chanting to create the illusion of the atmosphere of a wooden meditation hall, high in the Japanese mountains.

Accompanying himself on the Taiko drum, Chinese wind gong, Mokugyo (wood block) and Tibetan cymbals, the finished effect is enthrallingly realistic and a true spiritual experience.

TIBETAN JOURNEY
Zen Drumming
CB21, £11.75 CD

Superb meditational pieces with authentic instruments and deep spirituality.

A Buddhist disciple sets off on an epic personal pilgrimage from Nepal to the sacred city of Lhasa in Tibet, his journey powerfully depicted through Tibetan bowls, Taiko drum, Tincha and Tola bells.

THE TASTE OF TRANQUILLITY
CB23, £11.75 CD

The listener is taken through 4 Buddhist meditation techniques that Chris has taught for over 25 years. They are explained in a straightforward, easy to understand fashion that will, when applied, bring a feeling of calm and tranquillity to Buddhist and non-Buddhist alike.

FOUNDATIONS OF MEDITATION VIDEO
CB001 £12.99

REALISTIC TAROT VIDEO
CB002 £12.99

THE PURPOSE of this video is to introduce the student to a system of meditation that will bring not only a feeling of calm and stillness to the mind and body, but also form a solid and trustworthy foundation for any further meditation based practices that he/she may wish to embark on. As well as giving three meditation techniques, Chris also goes into all aspects of posture, including the use of a chair and sitting cross legged on the floor. Many other helpful tips covering such issues as, what time to meditate, where to meditate, etc., are also covered in detail.

This video is not only ideally suited to those with no prior knowledge of meditation, but can also be of great benefit to the more experienced student of meditation!

ON THIS VIDEO the student is shown how to use the Tarot as a means of embarking on a journey of self-exploration, leaving behind, and rising above what Chris calls the fortune telling depths that the ancient and mystical Tarot has been reduced to in certain areas. Chris explains, firstly, how each of the greater arcana of the Tarot deck represent inner aspects of the individual, before going on to meditation and pathworking with each card. He then moves on to instruct on how to do a reading (reflective meditation) on yourself and also how to use the cards when doing a reading (reflective meditation) for others.

It is not necessary to have any prior knowledge of Tarot to take up the practices laid out in this video!

PSYCHIC DEVELOPMENT VIDEO
CB005 £12.99

IF YOU ever wanted to try to develop your psychic skills then this video will show you how! In Chris's easy to follow method of teaching he takes the student through such skills as dowsing with pendulums and rods, developing the psychic energy centres in the body, how to use a ouija board and how to use water for scrying (visualising). He also goes into how to develop your psychic hearing or clairaudience, and instructs the student in how to travel back in time to look at past events in their life, both in this and past lives. As in all Chris's videos, his obvious knowledge of his subject comes over in his relaxed and sometimes humorous approach.

THE PURPOSE of this video is to instruct the student in the art of developing, or as Chris puts it, harnessing the positive energy needed to work with sick animals.

ANIMAL HEALING VIDEO
CB003 £12.99

The three techniques on the video will take the student, firstly, through the development of a meditation on becoming at one with all living creatures, before moving into the development and positive application of the healing energy, and ending with instruction in the use of instruments such as Tibetan singing bowls, gongs, etc., as an aid to the healing process. WARNING: Animal Healing is a complementary practice, not a replacement for veterinary treatment! A vet should always be consulted if any animal is sick or injured!

SOUND AND COLOUR HEALING VIDEO
CB006 £12.99

CHRIS HAS worked for many years with his own unique methods of colour and sound healing. On this video he explains in detail how to harness your own healing energy through colour meditation in a way that's refreshingly easy to understand and develop. He then takes the viewer through his methods of healing with sound aided by Tibetan singing bowls and gongs, etc., before moving on to show how to play and use the North African style frame drum as a tool for healing. All the practices explained on this video can be used as a complementary form of healing on both yourself and others.

ADVANCED MEDITATION VIDEO
CB004 £12.99

CHRIS TAKES the viewer beyond the foundations of meditation that he covered on video number one in the series, and instructs the student in how to take meditation into action through focusing on such areas as walking and eating. He then goes into the deeper aspects of insight meditation with a teaching aimed at overcoming our attachment to our own bodies, one of the greatest hindrances to really knowing who we are! Chris finishes the video with two techniques for taking your meditation into your sleep. This video is ideally suited to those who have made a start in meditation, and want to know more.

THE GENTLE ART OF MEDITATION FOR RELAXATION Video

CBOW001, 30mins, £12.99

Our video *The Gentle Art of Meditation for Relaxation* has been put together in a way that makes its application both easy to understand and a pleasure to do.

Chris's many years of teaching experience come through clearly on the film as he takes you through all the aspects of posture, technique, do's and don'ts, etc., finishing off with a carefully planned four week programme to get you started.

BOOKS BY CHRIS BURROWS

£4.95 EACH

- **Life's Crap, Then you Die**

  (The Foundations of Buddhism) CB922-9

- **Encounters on the Astral**

  (A Personal Record of Out of the Body Experiences)

Other titles by the same author.

Publication date to be announced.

- **Can Anybody Hear Me**

  (A Guide to Buddhist Chanting)

- **Look Before you Leap**

  (Advice on Entering the Spiritual Path)

- **Please Don't Eat Me**

  (Veganism, Compassion in Action)